The Shadow Dimension

Alan Gibbons ■ Dynamo

OXFORD
UNIVERSITY PRESS

TEAM X

Max, Cat, Ant and Tiger are four ordinary children with four extraordinary watches. When activated, their watches allow them to shrink to micro-size.

MAX — hologram communicator

CAT — magni-scope, tracking device

ANT — flip-up camera, video recorder

TIGER — warning light, torch

Previously ...

The watches were running low on power. Ant tried to recharge them using a machine that he had invented. However, during this process, something in the watches changed irrevocably.

When all the watches are synchronized, the micro-friends can travel through a rip in the fabric of space and time to other dimensions. Max, Cat, Ant and Tiger have become *rip-jumpers*.

However, there is a problem. The rip has become permanently stuck open ... in Tiger's wardrobe! This leaves Earth – our Earth – open to attack.

A woman called **Perlest** came through the rip saying she wanted to help. She told the children that they need to find the **Weaver**. Only he can seal the rip shut forever.

Now the children are trying to find Perlest's hidden thoughts – contained in **thought vials** – which will help them to track down the Weaver.

Chapter 1 – Why here?

Cat surveyed her surroundings and threw out her arms. 'Why here?' she said.

Max joined her at the top of the bare, blackened hill. He felt something crunch underfoot. 'You know why,' he said, wondering what he had trodden on. 'Perlest sent us to find the Weaver, to try and convince him to come back with us and save our dimension.'

'But here?' Cat said. 'I mean, just look at it. It's the most boring place we have ever been. It can't be right. There's nothing here, nothing at all.'

Ant leant on a nearby rock to catch his breath. Tiger stared across the bleak landscape. Everything was blanketed in a grey mist. Cat was right. There was nothing to see: no trees, no houses, no towers or skyscrapers, just murk and gloom and rock.

'It's dead,' Cat said. 'It's a dead, lifeless world.'

'We don't know if it's *lifeless*,' Ant pointed out. 'We need to explore first.'

'What's to explore?' Cat responded. 'Everywhere is the same. What are we supposed to find in a world that's nothing but rock and fog?' She kicked the ground. Dust rose in the air and a few shiny splinters flew up.

'Stop moaning!' Tiger snapped. 'We haven't been here very long.'

'You're a fine one to talk,' Cat said, folding her arms. 'You're always complaining. Besides, it feels like we've been stuck here forever, wandering around in this half-light.'

'Stop arguing,' Max said. 'Perlest says this place is important. She said that the last thought vial we found pointed us towards this dimension. We'll either find the Weaver here, another thought vial, or …'

'Or what?' Cat wasn't convinced. She turned her back on the others.

'You know *what*. Earth is in danger,' Tiger said. 'We have to find the Weaver. Only he can repair the rip in space and time that we created.'

'And how do we know that's true?' Cat yelled, turning back to face them, her eyes flashing. 'Only because *she* told us.'

'Look,' Max said, trying to calm things down. 'We've trusted Perlest so far, haven't we? Let's keep going and see what we can find.'

Cat glanced at the others.

'Well?' Max asked, resting a hand on her shoulder.

'Come on, Cat,' Tiger said. 'Just be patient a little bit longer.'

'Patient?' Cat chuckled. 'That's good coming from *you!* Since when were you the patient one?'

She was right. Tiger was the kind of impulsive person who acted first and thought second. Max and Ant burst out laughing. Their laughter sounded strange in the misty silence. The fog sucked it in and left a dull quiet behind.

Ant took a step forward. Something went *crunch*. He gazed up in the air. 'Has anybody seen the sun since we got here?'

'I haven't even seen the sky,' Max answered. 'The fog is too thick.'

That's when Ant stopped.

'What's up?' Max asked.

'If there isn't any sunlight,' Ant wondered out loud, 'how come we've still got shadows?'

Cat and Tiger looked at the ground.

'That *is* weird,' Tiger said.

Cat waved her arms; her shadow did the same. 'It's a perfectly ordinary shadow,' she said. 'Things must work differently here. It is a different dimension after all. The light must get through all this fog somehow.'

They continued to climb the steep slope, still puzzling about the strange shadows that appeared without light. After a while, the fog started to thin a little.

'Hey, there *is* a sun,' Ant said, pointing up at the watery glow high above them.

The thin, grainy light eddied through the mist, and the friends started to make out things they hadn't seen before. Here and there, dotted along the rocky ridges, were columns of rock two or three metres tall.

'They're like those things you find in caves,' Max said, 'you know, stalagmites and stalactites. I can never remember which is which.'

'Stalactites hang from the ceiling,' Ant said helpfully. 'These are like stalagmites. They rise from the ground.' He frowned. 'Something's wrong though.'

He had everyone's attention. 'First it was the shadows. Now there is …'

'What?' snapped Cat.

'I don't know exactly. I can't quite put my finger on it, but there is something weird about this dimension.'

Ant's words had made Cat take a closer look. She started to prowl round the nearest column. Finally, she worked it out. 'It's the shadows again,' she said. 'First we got shadows without sun. Now the shadow is a completely different shape from the thing that casts it.'

'That's impossible,' Ant protested.

'See for yourself,' Cat insisted. 'You've got to look really closely. The shadow isn't the same as the rock. See, it's more … human shaped.'

Tiger inspected the shadow. 'You're right. How can that be?'

Max reached out a hand. Very carefully he prodded the column. 'OK,' he said. 'This is getting weirder.'

'How come?'

'Feel it. It isn't rock.'

Cat reached out to touch the column. 'But if it isn't rock, what is it?'

The four friends puzzled over the strange material.

'I just wish the light was brighter,' Ant said. 'It's not as gloomy as it was at the bottom of the hill, but it's still hard to see properly.' He squinted at the column. 'This stuff's like a kind of crust. I'm sure there's something inside there.'

'Like what?' Max said.

Ant gave a sigh. 'I wish I knew. Maybe this is why Perlest sent us here.'

'This?' Cat said. 'How can it be? It's just a lump of rock. A lump of not-rock ... Oh, I don't know, a *lump*.'

'I don't get it either,' Ant said. 'Maybe I can use my watch.'

He fumbled with the green watch on his wrist.

'What are you doing?' Tiger asked.

'I'm going to film it,' Ant said. 'Maybe I can magnify a section, do something to clarify the image. It's worth a try.'

'Sounds good,' Max said. 'Give it a go.'

That's when Cat noticed something else. 'Look here.' She nudged a piece of glass with her foot.

'Careful,' Max said. 'Those splinters are sharp.' He scanned the earth. 'Hey, there are lots of them. I didn't notice them when the fog was really thick. They're everywhere.'

'It's as if somebody has smashed hundreds of windows to pieces,' Tiger said.

'Why would anyone do that?' Max wondered.

'Beats me,' Cat said. 'Everything is different here. There are shadows without bright sunlight, shadows the wrong shape, columns of *something*. Now all this glass. What's going on?'

'And that's not all,' Ant said. 'Look at this mist. It doesn't get you wet. I can't figure it out.'

Max glanced over at Tiger and froze. 'Tiger,' he said cautiously, 'look at your watch.'

It had started to flash red.

Red meant danger.

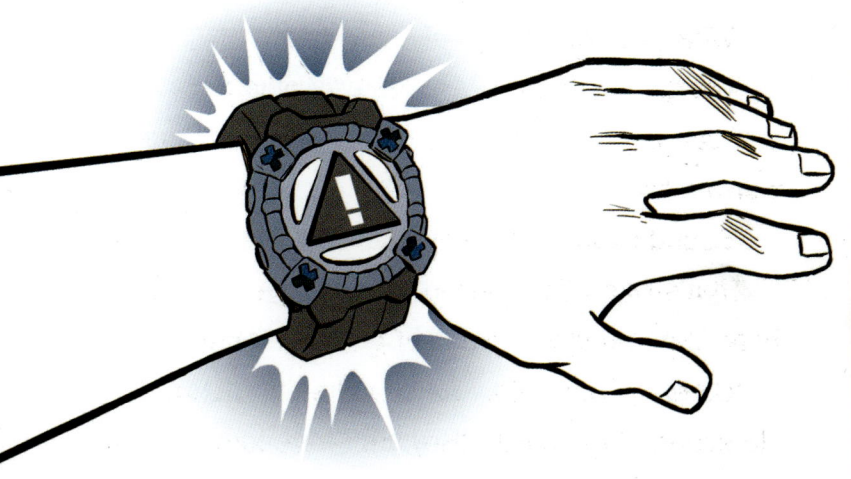

Chapter 2 – Red for danger

'Don't drop your guard,' Max whispered. 'We're not alone. I'm sure I saw movement over there.'

His friends turned. Instinctively, they reached for their watches, poised to shrink if necessary.

'I don't see anything,' Tiger said, peering through the yellowish mist. The thin sunlight still didn't provide much visibility.

'There!' Cat said. 'Max is right. I saw something move, too.' She had been complaining because the land of shadows was empty and dead. Now that there was some sign of life, her skin was prickling.

'Why doesn't it show itself?' Ant said anxiously. He called out, 'Is somebody there?'

They could hear the sound of dragging footsteps and straining, wheezing breaths.

'I've had enough of this,' Cat said, sounding braver than she felt.

'Cat, don't!' Max made a grab for her, but she had plunged into the mist. For a long moment, there wasn't a sound.

'Where is she?' Tiger hissed.

They waited, tense and alert.

Eventually, Cat reappeared. She had the most peculiar creature with her. It was hunched over, wrapped in a grey cloak, and its features were concealed by a hood that hung over its face.

'OK,' Cat said. 'Who are you and why are you following us?'

The creature pulled back its hood. It looked defeated, as if all the life had been sucked out of it. Its face was almost human-looking but as grey as the mist. It had the most enormous, startled eyes.

'Don't hurt me,' it whimpered. 'I mean you no harm.' It darted glances to its right and left. 'I wasn't following you. I was just looking for some food and water. I promised my brother I would find something to eat.'

'Where's this brother of yours?' Cat demanded. She didn't mean to snap, but she was scared. She noticed that the creature had straggly, thinning hair. Was it a *girl*?

'Back there,' it said. 'He was too tired to go on. I was supposed to find food and water, maybe somewhere to hide. We were going to meet at our rendezvous point. Don't hurt me.'

'Don't be afraid,' Max said. 'You're safe with us.'

'Who are you?' Cat asked.

For the first time, the creature gave a weak smile. 'I am Veta. I'm a twilighter.' She stroked the back of Cat's hand. 'I am a girl like you.'

Cat found herself smiling. There was nothing to fear from Veta.

'Why are you so frightened?' asked Max. 'What are you scared of?'

'The shadows,' Veta said. 'You must beware of your shadows.'

'What do you me–' began Ant, but before he could finish, Veta spun round, her eyes even wider than before.

'Did you hear that?' she said, her voice trembling.

'It's just the wind,' Tiger said. Then he considered for a moment. 'Hang on, there is no wind.'

The mist hardly moved at all. It hung limply, only drifting very slowly now and then like a sluggish tide.

Cat put a reassuring hand on Veta's arm. 'You said you were a twilighter ... What's a twilighter?'

'We are the people of the half-light,' Veta explained. 'Once, our world was beautiful. We had twelve hours of light and twelve hours of darkness. Then the mist came.'

'When did this happen?'

'Not so long ago. It is hard to say. Without darkness and light it is hard to keep track of time.'

'OK,' Cat said. 'Go on.'

'The mist swallowed the whole world. Now the sunlight hardly breaks through this evil fog. We twilighters grow weaker and weaker. There are fewer of us with each passing day.' Veta stared bitterly at the mist. 'These days, the sun breaks through for just two or three days a year. That's the only time we feel its warmth on our skin. For a few hours at least we are safe.'

'Safe from what?' Max asked.

'From *them*,' Veta answered. 'From the shadow creatures.'

'Shadow creatures?' repeated Tiger, stepping closer to his friends.

'They came with the mist. One day there will be nothing but the mist and we will all be imprisoned by the shadows. Then they will have what they want, a world of endless darkness.'

'How many more twilighters are there?' Ant asked.

'There are only a few of us left.' She wiped away a tear with the back of her wrinkled hand. 'When they catch us, it will be the end.'

Cat examined Veta's face. 'Why do you hide your face under that hood?'

'I was once pretty like you', Veta said, 'before the world grew dark. I had fine, dark hair like yours. Now I am grey and wrinkled … and my hair is falling out.' She suddenly grew tense. 'Listen, there is something I must tell you …'

She didn't finish her sentence. There was a sound like the rush of the wind.

Veta cried out, 'It's them!' Her eyes flashed. 'They're coming. Watch your shadows. I have to go back to my brother. He will be waiting for me. He will be afraid.' She started to stumble away, fleeing as quickly as she could.

'Veta,' Cat shouted, staggering after her. 'Come back. You're safe with us.' She could hear Veta's dragging footsteps just ahead of her. The mist was closing in. As Cat crept forward, trying to find the twilighter, she heard a cry of fright.

'Veta!' Cat reached into the mist. 'Veta, are you there?'

There was no answer.

'Veta, talk to me.' She inched forward. Veta's cry had been close. She had to be somewhere nearby. 'Veta?'

Then she felt something. It was one of the columns. A thought occurred to Cat, but she pushed it away. *No, it can't be.* She stared at the ground, at the muddy shadow cast by the weak sunlight. It was a figure. She could make out the shape. The figure was somehow familiar. *It can't be.*

Finally, the others caught up with her.

'Did you find her?' Tiger asked. 'Did you find Veta?'

Cat was standing with her head bowed.

'I think so,' Cat said, haunted by her thoughts.

Tiger looked over Cat's shoulder. 'I don't get it. Where is she?'

'You won't find her over there,' Cat said.

Max scratched his head. 'Am I missing something here? Cat, you're talking in riddles. Where is she?'

Ant spoke next. 'I think I understand.'

'Understand?' Tiger said. 'Understand what? Why are you all playing silly games? Will somebody explain this to me?'

Ant showed him the image on his watch. 'There is a body inside that column back there.'

'There is a body inside this one, too,' Cat added. She ran her fingertips over the surface of the column. 'This is Veta.'

Chapter 3 – Beware your shadows

'But how?' Tiger demanded. 'How can this be Veta? She was here just a few moments ago. How could she turn into a lump of rock in just a few seconds? It doesn't make any sense.'

'This isn't rock,' Ant said. 'It's just an outer casing, like the crust of a pie. It's a cage, a prison.'

'So are you telling us Veta is inside?' Max asked. 'Is she dead or alive?'

'Alive, I think,' Ant responded. 'I hope. Look at this.' The other three crowded round and peered at his watch's small screen. Ant played the recording. 'See the dark, shadowy thing in the middle? I think that's the living person inside. It's probably another of those twilighters, somebody just like Veta. If you keep watching, you can see it twitch. There!'

'Yes,' Cat said. 'I saw it move.' She turned to the column next to them. Her face was tight and scared. 'We have to get Veta out. It's a living death!'

'How?' Max wondered out loud. 'Maybe we can break off this crust …'

'Don't be in such a hurry,' Ant said. 'It might hurt Veta. She's alive. So are all these other columns. The best thing we can do is leave them like this until we can figure out how to get them out safely.'

'So all those columns we've seen', Tiger said, eyes wide with fright, 'they're all captured twilighters?'

'That's my guess,' Ant said.

'But why?' Max said. 'Why would anybody do this? What's the point of keeping living things in these columns?'

'I still don't have enough information to go on,' Ant replied. 'I'm trying to work it out. I do know one thing. We're all in danger. Don't you remember what Veta said? She told us that the shadows are dangerous.'

'That's right,' Cat said, scanning the ground around her. 'She told us to be wary of our own shadows. Whatever did this to her must have crept into her shadow.'

Tiger shivered and looked down at his shadow. 'We could be turned into rocks, too.'

Suddenly, none of them felt safe.

'Listen!' Ant said.

'What is it?' Max asked.

Tiger pointed. 'I can hear it, too. There!'

It was just as before. They could hear the same dragging footsteps as they had earlier, the same wheezing breath.

'It's Veta!' Cat exclaimed, eyes sparkling. 'We were wrong. That column isn't her, after all.' She took a step forward. She was so happy. Veta was safe. She saw the shadowy shape of her new friend forming in the mist. She could see the grey hood. 'Look, it's her.'

But when the twilighter appeared, Cat's face fell in disappointment. The face that peered out from the hood was unfamiliar. It wasn't Veta.

'Who are you?' Max asked.

The twilighter pulled back his hood. 'I'm Zorb,' he said. 'I'm looking for my sister. We were supposed to meet at the rendezvous point but she never showed up. Have you seen her?'

Instinctively, Cat turned towards the column.

Zorb understood immediately. He threw himself forward and wrapped his arms round it. He leaned his forehead against the object imprisoning his sister.

'No,' he sobbed. 'Not Veta. We should never have split up. I was tired. I had to rest. She went looking for food and water. We were on the run from the shadow creatures. I told her not to go on by herself, but she has always been braver than me. I begged her.' He started to beat his head against the column that held Veta. 'I am too late.'

'We should get moving,' Max said. 'It's dangerous to stay in one place.' They started to walk away from the column Veta was trapped in with leaden hearts.

Zorb didn't follow. 'Who are you, anyway?' he called after them. 'How do I know I can trust you? You could be working with the shadow creatures.'

'We are travellers,' Cat said, turning to face him. 'We didn't know about the twilighters or the shadow creatures or any of this until a short time ago. We still don't really understand what's happening here.'

Zorb gazed at her for a few moments, wondering whether he could trust her. 'Very well,' he said eventually. 'I believe you.' He shuffled after them. 'But what made you come here? Why would you visit a terrible place like this one?'

'We are looking for something,' Max explained. 'A thought vial. It belongs to a woman called Perlest. She sent us here to find it.'

Zorb scratched his head. 'Perlest? Do I know that name? I'm not sure. It is hard to remember. The mist does that to you. You forget things. You forget who you are. We weren't always called twilighters. We were … No, it's gone.'

Zorb was absorbed in thought for a few moments. Then he spoke again. 'The shadow creatures are afraid of the light. We have been waiting so long for the dawn of a new day.'

'When is it?' Ant asked. 'When is dawn?'

'Soon,' Zorb said. 'I used to know exactly, but I find it hard to remember. It could be weeks or days or perhaps only hours. Do you see the way the glow of the sun is getting stronger?'

'He's right,' Cat said. 'It's getting lighter.'

'Poor Veta,' Zorb said. 'She only had to stay away from the creatures a little while longer, but they found her.'

'If we could find a way to defeat the shadow creatures,' Ant said, 'maybe we could free your sister and the others?'

'There is a way,' Zorb said.

'How do we do it?'

Before Zorb could answer, there was a blast of cold wind.

'Oh, no!' said Tiger, spinning round, looking at the ground. 'They're back.'

'Zorb!' Ant cried, grabbing the twilighter's sleeve. 'Tell me how we stop the shadow creatures.'

'They came for Veta,' Zorb said, eyes popping with fear. 'Now they're coming for the rest of us.'

There it was again, a sound like the wind.

'They're going to get me,' Zorb cried.

'Nobody's going to get you,' Cat said sternly. 'Stick with us and you'll be safe.'

Zorb was trembling.

'You've got to calm down,' Cat told him.

Zorb wasn't listening. His eyes were wild. 'Run!' he yelled.

The wind that wasn't wind blew again, but it didn't shake the mist. All five of them ran over the glass-strewn ground, but they were losing each other in the gloom. Then Cat heard a cry. It was Tiger. She stopped and turned in his direction.

'Tiger?' she called. 'Tiger, where are you?'

Cat stumbled towards the cry, shoes crunching on the shards of glass that littered the ground. She stepped over one of the streams that cut through the rocks. 'Tiger, talk to me.'

Instead she heard Max. 'He's over here.'

Cat followed the sound of his voice. Finally, she could make out the blurry outlines of Max and Ant in the mist. 'Where's Tiger?' she asked. 'Is he with you?' As she got nearer, she said, 'Max? Ant? Where's Zorb? Where's Tiger?'

Neither of them said a word. She made her way towards them, more and more certain of what she would find.

Finally, the mist cleared a little and a ray of sunshine broke through. It lit the ground where Max and Ant were standing. They were on either side of a column.

'Oh no,' she said. 'Tell me it isn't him.'

Then she saw the telltale sign. Just visible through the surface of the column was a winking, red light coming from Tiger's watch.

Red for danger.

Chapter 4 – Then there were three

'Listen!' Max cried.

There it was again, the rush of wind. For the first time they heard the voices of their pursuers.

Find them. Capture them.

'It's the shadow creatures,' Cat whispered. 'There are more of them.'

'We can't stay here,' Max said. 'We'll all end up like Tiger.'

'We can't leave him!' Cat protested. 'He's our friend.'

'We're not going to leave him,' Max said, tugging at her sleeve. 'As soon as we know how to free him, we'll come back.'

'Max is right,' Ant said. 'We'll be no good to him if we end up trapped ourselves. We've got to escape and find somewhere to hide. We need some rest and time to decide what to do.'

'There is no hiding place,' Cat cried. 'You heard what Veta and Zorb said. They're always on the run.'

'Where is Zorb?' Ant said. 'Has he been captured?'

Nobody had an answer. The rush of wind came again. This time it was closer.

'We can't just stand here,' Max said firmly.

The noise was getting louder.

'Move!' Max ordered.

They continued to stumble through the mist, without any idea of where they were going. Their only instinct was to escape from the creatures that were following them.

'Stick close together,' Max told his friends. 'We've lost Tiger. We don't want to lose anyone else.'

'But where are we going?' Cat panted. 'How will we ever find our way back?' She stopped. 'We're lost.'

Ant paused and listened. 'I can't hear the shadow creatures,' he said. 'We seem to have outrun them … for now.'

'But what do we do?' Cat demanded. 'We can't just *keep* running.'

Before any of them could say anything else, there was another noise. They tensed.

'Did you hear that?' Max asked.

'It's over there,' Ant said. 'To our left.'

Cat searched the mist. 'Shadow creatures?'

Ant shook his head. 'I don't think so. It doesn't sound the same.'

Then they heard the familiar sound of a dragging walk and wheezing breath. Zorb had returned. 'You're safe ... good,' he grunted. Then he looked around. 'Hang on, where's your friend?'

Max just shook his head.

'I'm sorry.'

Cat swallowed and changed the subject. 'Did you come looking for us?'

Zorb nodded. 'I don't like being on my own. Veta was always there to help me. I wish I could be brave like her. Follow me. I've found somewhere for us to rest.'

They followed him for a few minutes until they came to the mouth of a cave. When they peered inside, they could see the glow of a fire.

'We will be safe in here,' Zorb said. 'It was where I was supposed to rendezvous with Veta. The fire will keep the shadow creatures away … for a while at least.' He led them inside and rolled a boulder across the entrance.

Max went over and tried to push the boulder. It didn't budge. 'You must be really strong,' he said.

Zorb shrugged his shoulders. 'It didn't help Veta, did it?' He sat down next to the fire and rubbed his bony hands. 'There are caves like this all over these hills,' he said. 'They are the only places where we can sleep.'

'How long have you been living like this?' Max asked, joining Zorb next to the fire. He tried to imagine what it would be like, always a fugitive, always afraid.

Zorb shrugged. 'A few years. It's hard to remember. We move from cave to cave. We stay as long as we can before hunger and thirst drive us out into the mist. The shadow creatures just wait until we come out. We always hope the dawn will come and give us new strength. The shadow creatures fear the light. It is our only hope.'

'Why are the shadow creatures afraid of the light?' Ant asked. 'Light creates shadows. It's all very odd.'

Cat sat down and looked at the others. 'Maybe we should stop thinking of the shadow creatures as … shadows,' she said. 'Shadows aren't the same here. We've already worked that out. Here you still get shadows when there's hardly any light.' She had everyone's attention. 'OK, this is what I think. The shadow creatures jump into their victims' shadows for camouflage. It's how they hunt. They're nothing to do with shadows themselves.'

Ant stared at her, nodding slowly. 'You might have something there.'

'It's like a big jigsaw,' Cat said. 'If only we had all the pieces.'

Ant was quiet for a while. 'Pieces. A jigsaw of pieces … What if the pieces are made of broken glass? That's it, Cat! There's a connection between the shadow creatures and the broken glass. We've just got to work out what it is.'

Max turned to Zorb. 'Try to think back to how it started,' he said. 'Have you ever seen what the shadow creatures look like?'

'It's hard,' Zorb said. 'The mist makes us weak. It takes our memories away. Sometimes I hardly know who I am anymore.'

'Just try,' Cat said. 'Please.'

'Anything,' Max said. 'Try to think of anything that can help us.'

For a long time, Zorb didn't say a word. Then he looked up.

'There is something,' he said. 'I remember the day they came. A great fog rolled into our town. We didn't know what it was or where it came from. It covered everything. You couldn't see where to go. Then we heard them. It was as if a thousand winds were blowing all at the same time.' Zorb stopped and stared into the fire.

'Is there anything else?' Max prompted.

Zorb nodded. 'I remember the noise. All the windows exploded. Yes … every single window blew out. Then the mirrors in the houses smashed to pieces. It was as if invisible hammers were destroying them all at once. Nothing made of glass was left.'

He lowered his voice to a whisper, chuckling. 'But we saved some of the mirrors. We took them ...' He seemed surprised by his own memories. 'We took them to the Great Waterfall. We hid them in a cave behind it.'

Cat was excited. 'Why did you do that?'

Ant knew this was important. 'Yes, why did you need the mirrors? What were you going to do with them?'

Zorb put his face in his hands. 'I don't remember.'

'Try,' Max said. 'Please try. This might tell us how to beat the shadow creatures and rescue Tiger, Veta and the others. If you could just remember, you might get your world back.'

Zorb wracked his brains, but no matter how hard he tried, he could not remember. 'I'm sorry. That's all I know. Why can't I be more like Veta? I am so tired.' Zorb curled up on the floor of the cave and buried his head in his arms. He was half-asleep, but he was still mumbling to himself. 'So tired.'

'We should let him sleep,' Cat said. 'Maybe when he wakes up, he might remember more.'

Zorb was already snoring.

'I don't see what else we can do,' Max said.

Chapter 5 – Zorb remembers

'Light and dark,' Zorb cried, waking everyone up. 'Objects and shadows, things and their reflections. That's it!'

'You remember!' Cat exclaimed. 'Listen, everybody. Zorb's thought of something.'

Max and Ant shook the stiffness from their bodies and crowded round Zorb.

'It is so long since I slept properly,' Zorb said. 'It has helped me get some of my strength back. Listen carefully. This is what you need to know. Those creatures – the shadow creatures – they live inside the mist, hidden from sight. It isn't real mist. Have you noticed how it doesn't make you damp? It's something they bring with them. It's their home. They use it for cover, to leap into the shadows of living things.'

'Yes, we'd guessed most of that,' Ant said. 'What else?'

Zorb was excited. His huge eyes were glistening. 'I know about the columns.'

DIMENSION 6972
THE SHADOW CREATURES

The shadow creatures are parasites. They use stone-like columns to imprison people, then they draw energy from their victims in small doses. This way, the shadow creatures use their victims like batteries, storing them until they need the energy. Eventually, they will drain all the life force from their victims.

The shadow creatures are able to move between dimensions. Everywhere they go, they suck the life out of the people they find there. When they have drained all the energy from that dimension, they move on to the next.

WEAKNESS:

The most effective way to defeat the shadow creature is using light or their reflections.

- **column prison**
- **up to 3 metres tall**
- **shadow creature**

After Zorb had explained the purpose of the columns, he paused. 'But I was wrong about something,' Zorb said. 'Yes, I remembered it wrong.'

'What's that?' Max asked, leaning forward.

'The smashing of the glass,' Zorb answered. 'That wasn't in the beginning. No, that came later.'

'I don't understand,' Cat said.

'I do,' Ant exclaimed. 'You used glass as a weapon against them, didn't you?'

'Yes!' Zorb cried. 'Yes, we fought back. Back then, the mist wasn't so thick. At first we could see the outlines of the shadow creatures. One of them saw its reflection in a mirror. It screamed and turned to dust. That's how we knew we could fight them. We made them look at their own reflections. They can't stand it, you see. If the creatures see themselves, they die.'

'How did they smash the mirrors without seeing their reflections?' Cat asked.

'That's why they need so much energy,' Zorb said. 'They have to use blasts of sound to destroy the mirrors from far away.'

'So that explains why there's glass everywhere,' Ant said. 'They knew they had to destroy it to protect themselves.'

'Yes, that's it. That's it!' agreed Zorb.

'What else can you tell us?'

'A few of us tried to resist,' Zorb continued, 'but we were too late. They were too strong. They were everywhere.'

'You said something about a Great Waterfall,' Ant reminded him. 'Your people hid the mirrors there.'

'That's right,' Zorb said. 'We managed to hide a few mirrors behind the tumbling waters.'

'So why haven't you gone back for them already?' Cat asked. 'I mean, if the mirrors are the only way to fight the shadow creatures, why didn't you go back to the Great Waterfall?'

Zorb lowered his head.

'The mist makes us weak,' he said. 'The shadow creatures have captured most of us. They've caught all the brave ones who wanted to fight. That leaves the cowards like me.'

'Stop saying you're a coward,' Cat said. 'You can be brave like Veta. I know you can.'

'I'm not brave at all. I can't help you any more than I have,' Zorb said. He pointed down the hill. 'I can't go with you to the Great Waterfall.'

Ant sighed. 'OK. I get it.'

'Well, I don't,' Cat said. 'What's the problem? Why don't we just go and get them?'

'The mist is thicker further down the valley,' Ant explained. 'That's right, isn't it Zorb?'

Zorb nodded. 'Yes, the mist is thicker there,' he said, 'it's where the shadow creatures gather. If we want to get the mirrors, we have to go where our enemies are strongest.'

For a time, everyone stared at the ground. It had been hard enough to avoid the shadow creatures in the hills. It would be even worse down in the valley.

'Just a minute,' Ant said. 'We're forgetting something. Come on, all of you, let's roll back this boulder.'

They heaved, but it wouldn't budge.

'Zorb,' Ant said. 'You're stronger than us. Give us a hand.'

With Zorb's help, they rolled back the boulder and stepped outside.

'See,' Ant said, 'it's getting lighter all the time. Dawn is almost here. Even down in the valley we will be able to see enough to find our way. If we can reach the Great Waterfall and retrieve those mirrors, we can show the shadow creatures their reflections.'

'It's still dangerous,' Max said. 'We'd better *you know what,* too.'

Cat and Ant nodded. They knew he meant they should shrink to stay safe.

'What about Zorb?' whispered Cat. They had sworn long ago to keep their watches and their shrinking powers secret.

'I think we need to make an exception to our rule,' said Max. The others nodded. 'Zorb,' he said addressing the twilighter directly, 'will you come with us? We could do with your help.'

'I don't know,' Zorb said. 'It's very dangerous.'

'What if we promise to keep you safe?' said Ant.

'But how will you do that?' he asked, uncertain.

'You'll have to trust us,' Ant told him. 'What do you say?'

A troubled smile appeared on Zorb's face. 'I say we get those shadow creatures,' he said, trying his best to sound brave. 'You're right. It's Veta's only chance. Let's go.'

The four of them made their way down the hillside towards the valley, keeping to the brightest patches of light as far as possible; the sky above them was clearing. It was only when they reached the top of the valley that Max stopped the group.

'OK,' he said, reaching for his watch. 'Zorb, hold on to Ant's arm.'

Zorb did as he was instructed and the three children turned the dials on their watches and shrank to micro-size.

Cat laughed when she saw Zorb's face. 'You get used to it!'

Zorb gasped. 'We're … tiny!'

'We're safer than we were at normal size,' Max told him. 'At least I hope we are.'

'How long before dawn?' Ant asked.

'Not long now,' Zorb told him. 'We have to be quick. We must not waste this opportunity. We will only be able to show the shadow creatures their reflections while it is bright enough.'

They started to run, jogging down the slope.

'Stay away from the glass,' Cat said casually. 'It could be really dangerous when we are this size.'

Zorb's eyes grew even wider. He was trying to be brave, but it was all too overwhelming.

It was still dark and misty at the bottom of the valley. They started to hear the distinctive sound of the shadow creatures, the fast rush of wind.

'Listen,' Zorb said. 'There are so many of them. There are dozens.'

'More like hundreds,' said Ant. 'The wind is really loud! Where's the Great Waterfall?'

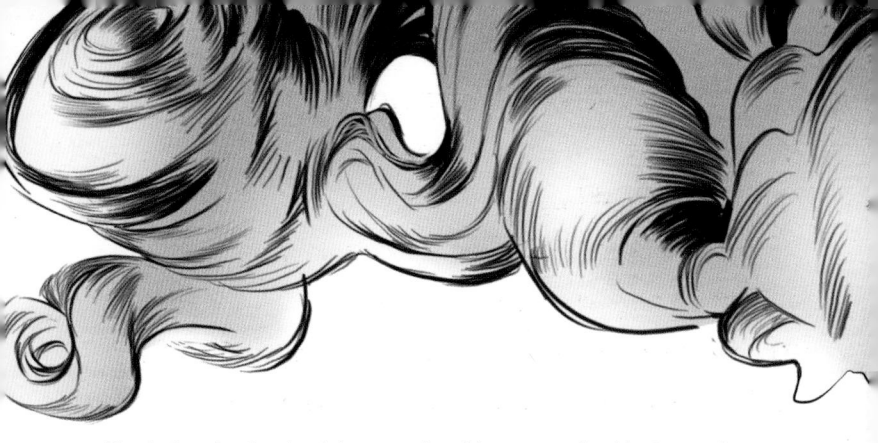

Zorb had started to panic. He was darting anxious glances left and right. He couldn't think.

'This way,' Zorb said. 'No, no, that way.'

'Make your mind up,' Cat said.

Zorb clawed at his head. 'It's no good!' he cried. 'I can't think.'

'Zorb,' Ant said. 'We haven't got much time.'

Zorb sank to his knees. 'I can't do it. I've let you down.'

'Zorb, pull yourself together,' Cat said. 'We need you. Veta needs you.'

That just made Zorb more nervous.

'This is no good,' Max said. 'We're confusing him. Everybody stop talking. Maybe we can *hear* the waterfall.'

Sure enough, when they stopped talking, they could just about hear the water in the distance, audible above the sound of rushing wind.

Chapter 6 – The attack

The wind was stronger now. The shadow creatures were massing as they advanced towards them, speeding through the mist.

'They're coming!' Zorb cried.

Max turned to his right and saw a blurry outline in the mist. 'No … they're already here.'

'So why are we just waiting for them to take us?' Cat demanded angrily. 'We know the waterfall is over there. We'll have to return to normal size to outrun them.'

Max adjusted his watch then grabbed hold of Zorb's arm. 'Let's go,' he ordered.

As soon as they were back to normal size, they sprinted across the earth, as the shadow creatures swept ever closer.

Once more, the friends heard the creatures' eerie voices: **We have them.**

'Not so fast,' Max shouted to Cat. 'Zorb can't keep up.'

'Go on without me,' Zorb told him. 'Find the mirrors. It's the only way to save this world.'

Even as he spoke, the rush of the wind grew louder and louder. Cat was in the lead. She heard the cry behind her and spun round, just in time to see Max throwing himself in front of Zorb to protect him. Then both Zorb and Max vanished into the murk.

'Where did they go?' Cat cried.

'Keep going!' Ant said, pushing Cat on.

'But they might have got Max and Zorb! We can't leave them!'

Ant looked grim. 'We can't go back to find out either. Come on!'

Cat felt something trying to pull her back, as if tugging at her shadow. She put on an extra spurt of speed.

Get them.

Cat was running as fast as she could down the slope, zigzagging all the time to make it harder for the shadow creatures to jump into her shadow. Suddenly, the toe of her shoe hit something and she pitched forward.

'Are you all right?' Ant asked, skidding to a stop behind her.

'I'm fine,' she said, crossly. She got up and brushed off the grit that stuck to her palms. Her hands were grazed but otherwise she was OK.

There! came the sinister voices of the shadow creatures.

'It's no good,' Ant said, shoulders slumping. 'The shadow creatures are too strong. We're outnumbered!'

'Don't you dare give up,' Cat said. 'You're starting to sound like Zorb. It's the mist – it's affecting you.' Cat grabbed him by the arm and started to drag him down the hill. 'You listen to me. We're going to find those mirrors and then we're going to beat the shadow creatures and set our friends free. Do you understand?'

Ant concentrated on the ground in front of him, too out of breath to reply.

'I need you, Ant,' Cat carried on. 'Max isn't the only practical one. You're good at working things out. It's you and me now. The others are relying on us. So what do you say?'

'Can't ... talk ... just ... run.'

Cat smiled to herself.

The pair made their way towards the sound of the Great Waterfall.

'I can still hear them,' Ant panted, as they ran.

'Try not to listen,' Cat hissed. 'Keep your eyes on the ground in front of you.'

They kept going. Soon they could hear the thundering sound of water pounding rock.

'We must be close,' said Ant.

Cat turned to glance at Ant. 'Behind you!' she cried, looking over his shoulder.

Ant spun round in time to see a dark form rise up from his shadow. 'No!' He squeezed his eyes shut, bracing himself for what was to come, expecting to be imprisoned in one of the strange stone-like columns.

Instead, there was a high-pitched scream and a sound like rain on a metal roof. Ant opened his eyes. The shadow creature was gone. He brushed himself down. 'I'm covered in dirt.'

'That's not dirt,' Cat said, amazed. 'That's one of the shadow creatures. You turned it to dust. I saw it happen. How did you do it?'

Ant shook his head, mystified. 'I don't know. I didn't do any–' Then he smiled, realizing what had happened. 'My glasses!'

'What?'

'Can you see yourself in my glasses?'

'Yes I can, just,' Cat replied. 'Why …?' Then she too understood. 'It saw its reflection! Ant, we've got a secret weapon. If they come, you just keep looking right at them.'

Ant wasn't afraid any more. Every time one of the shadow creatures came near, he turned so that they saw their reflection in his glasses. Three times they came. Three times they turned to dust.

'Don't take your eyes off them,' Cat said.

'Don't worry,' Ant told her. 'I know what I'm doing.' He glanced back at the line of hills behind them. 'Look, it's getting lighter all the time. The sun is about to rise. It's nearly dawn.'

Cat gave him a broad smile. 'We've done it!' she shouted, above the noise of cascading water. 'We're right on top of the waterfall. We'll …'

At that moment, the shadow creatures chose to attack again. Ant turned to face them. One after another, he turned them to dust. When it was over, he looked back to his friend. Cat was gone.

'Cat!' Ant yelled. 'Where are you?' Horror seized him. The shadow creatures must have got her, too.

He was the only one left.

Chapter 7 – **The Great Waterfall**

Ant took a few hesitant steps and peered over the ledge. It was now light enough to see what was in front of him. He was standing at the top of the waterfall, staring down at the river below. The thought of falling off the vertiginous cliff into the river made him feel dizzy. He hated heights. He crept along the edge of the cliff, gazing down at the roaring water as it cascaded into the river.

'The cave must be down there', he told himself, 'behind all that water.' He listened for the shadow creatures, but he couldn't hear anything above the roar of the waterfall. His heart pounded with fright. Then he clenched his fists. 'Pull yourself together, Ant,' he murmured. 'You've come this far. Don't give up now.' A shaft of sunlight broke through the mist and warmed his face. 'They're not going to beat me. I won't give in. I won't!'

He found a path down the cliff. The rocks were smooth and slippery. The dawn light was gaining strength all the time. Its golden rays gleamed on the rocks. This climb would have been impossible in the half-light. Now, as long as he took it easy and placed his feet carefully, it didn't pose much of a problem.

'Easy does it,' he reassured himself.

He saw a couple of misty shadows, but all he had to do was turn his head towards them and the shadow creatures would retreat. *They're scared of me,* he thought.

Down, down, down, he climbed. At last he could discern the entrance to the cave behind the water. *Nearly there,* he thought, *but what if the shadow creatures know about the mirrors? What if they have already found them and smashed them to bits?*

He was so tired. His legs were trembling. He had to concentrate hard so that he didn't lose his footing. *Come on, Ant. Just a few steps further.*

Now, the shadow creatures were swooping around him. The noise from the wind and the water was deafening. He had to twist and turn as he picked his way down the rocky descent. From time to time, one of them would see itself reflected in his glasses and turn to dust, but there were so many of them. *Too many,* Ant thought. He couldn't keep them all at bay. Any moment now, one of them would jump into his shadow and it would all be over.

'Get back!' he yelled. 'Leave me alone!'

He scrambled further down the cliff path. Twice, he almost tumbled off, but he managed to hold on to the slippery rock. He took a deep breath, ducked behind the tumbling water at the bottom and reached the cave that lay behind it. The shadow creatures seemed to gather outside the entrance to the cave, away from the water.

'Of course! They might glimpse their reflections in the pool at the bottom of the waterfall!'

He was feeling more confident. But where were the mirrors? Then his shoes crunched on glass and his heart turned to stone. *No,* he thought, *it can't be.* The floor of the cave was strewn with broken glass. The mirrors! Somebody must have smashed them all.

'No,' he groaned. 'No!'

Just then, one of the shadow creatures slid into the cave, taking its chance with the water in a desperate attempt to capture the last of their prey. More followed. Any moment now, one of them would jump into his shadow.

'Go away!' Ant screamed.

The shadow creatures were closing in. Sheltered in the cave from the noise of the water, the sound of the sinister creatures was louder than ever, making it difficult for Ant to think.

'Get off me!' Ant yelled, putting his hands to his ears. 'Get away!'

Then he heard another voice.

'Yeah, get away from him.'

It was Cat! That wasn't all. She was holding up a mirror. It was almost as big as she was. She turned it towards the creatures.

Suddenly, the entire cave was filled with eerie, high-pitched screams. Cat pointed the mirror at the shadow creatures and, one after another, they started to turn to dust around her.

'Take that!' she shouted. 'This is for Tiger.' She strode forward, pointing the mirror at the shadow creatures, turning them to dust. 'This is for Max. And this is for Zorb and Veta.' The rest of the creatures started to retreat.

'Cat,' Ant said, gasping with relief. 'I thought they'd got you.'

'I fell,' Cat explained. 'I went right over the edge of the waterfall and landed in the pool at the bottom.'

Ant was almost lost for words. All he could say was, 'You're wet.'

'Of course I'm wet, I fell in the water,' Cat growled. 'When I climbed out, I found the cave, just like you did.'

'Did we do it?' Ant wondered. 'Did we destroy the shadow creatures?'

'No,' Cat said. 'Not all of them. Listen, Ant. We're not safe yet. We've got to find every single one of the shadow creatures before they cause the mist to make it dark again.'

'There are only two of us left,' Ant said. 'How can we do it on our own?'

'I don't know, but we've got to find a way,' Cat said. 'It's the only way we can beat them.'

Ant nodded, then pointed to the mirror she was

holding. 'Are there any more mirrors like that? If we're going to get all the shadow creatures, I think we'll need more than one.'

'There are a few,' Cat said. 'I found them hidden under the dirt and moss at the back of the cave.'

Cat took Ant to where the rest of the mirrors were stashed. There were twenty in total, all wrapped in cloth to protect them. They were resting on a crude, wooden trolley with ropes attached.

Ant examined the mirrors. 'How are we going to get them back up the cliff? We'll never manage to drag this lot.'

Cat looked disappointed. 'Well, we've got to try.'

They started to drag the trolley towards the mouth of the cave. They hadn't gone far when Cat heard something. The shadow creatures were talking to each other.

In here. They're here.

Ant could see sinister shapes looming out of what was left of the mist.

'What are they doing?' he said. 'Oh no!'

'What's wrong?' Cat demanded.

Then the cave was plunged into total darkness. The shadow creatures had rolled a large rock over the entrance. They were trapped.

Chapter 8 – Pitch black

No matter how hard they tried, Cat and Ant couldn't budge the boulder.

'We could use our watches to shrink to micro-size,' Ant suggested.

'What would be the point?' Cat said. 'I can't see any gaps we could escape through. Besides, we can't shrink *all* the mirrors and we're going to need them all to fight the shadow creatures. If we don't fight them, we won't last very long. Have you got any other ideas?'

Ant was quiet for a few moments, then he shook his head. 'I haven't got a clue.'

'We've got to do something,' Cat said. 'We might only have a few hours to find the remaining shadow creatures. Come on, Ant, think. There's got to be something we can do.'

Ant buried his head in his hands. 'I'm trying.'

For a few minutes, neither of them said a word. Then Cat grabbed Ant by the arm.

'Listen.'

There was the rumble of the boulder being rolled back from the cave mouth.

'They're coming back,' Cat said, grabbing the nearest mirror. 'They're going to attack.'

Ant armed himself with a mirror as well. But, when the boulder rolled aside, it wasn't the shadow creatures they saw. It was Zorb.

'We thought the creatures had got you,' Cat said.

Zorb shook his head in sorrow. 'That was Max.'

'You came for us', Ant said, 'even though you were afraid.'

Zorb nodded. 'Max saved me. I owe him.'

'Can you help us to pull the mirrors up the path?' Cat asked.

A few minutes later, the friends were slowly ascending the steep slope of the valley. Something made Ant turn and look behind him, but he quickly wished he hadn't. The shadow creatures were pursuing them, in a cloud of grey mist.

'They daren't attack us now we have the mirrors,' Cat said.

'That's not all,' Ant said. 'They're afraid of seeing their reflections in the river.'

'That must be why my people chose this place to store the mirrors,' Zorb said.

It was a long climb to the top of the waterfall, but with the rising sun on their faces they felt invigorated. Finally they clambered to the top of the steep path.

Ant looked out at the valley. 'I have an idea,' he said. He instructed Cat and Zorb to set up the mirrors at intervals along one side of the valley.

Ant set up another two mirrors angled differently to the others. 'Just a bit to the left I think.' Then he tilted one of the mirrors back ninety degrees. 'If I've got my calculations right then ...'

'Then what?' asked Cat, jogging back to Ant.

'Be patient,' he replied, looking at his watch then up into the sky towards the sun. 'You're starting to sound like Tiger!'

After exactly two-and-a-half minutes, just as Ant had calculated, the sunlight hit the first of the mirrors; the light reflected on to the next mirror which shone out on to the next and the next. Soon, all twenty mirrors were shining into the valley, dazzling it with light.

The mist started to disappear as the shadow creatures turned to dust en masse. When the valley was clear, the friends repositioned the mirrors to cover more and more of the land.

There were five or six columns on the hillside above the valley. As the sun hit them, the columns started to crack.

'Did you see that?' Zorb cried.

Cat grinned at him as the captives inside stumbled out.

'They're coming back to life!' Ant said.

They retraced their steps. The next column started to crack and a familiar fist punched its way through the hard casing. It was Max.

'Max!' Cat yelled in delight. 'Don't you ever do that to us again!'

'Get turned into stone, you mean?' he said, stretching his aching limbs.

'I meant scare us like that!'

As they carried on retracing their path, they eventually found Tiger and Veta. As soon as she was free, Zorb rushed forward and hugged his sister. All six of them armed themselves with the mirrors. Everywhere they went, the trapped twilighters came back to life.

'The shadow creatures are weakening,' Ant said. 'They're nothing without their human power sources.'

Soon the remaining shadow creatures had retreated inside a dense, swirling whirlpool of mist.

'It's like a mist fortress,' Max said.

'It's their last stand,' Tiger said.

The four friends and their twilighter allies surrounded the shadow creatures. They created a circle of glittering mirrors. There was a huge roar of wind, then the mist vanished. Every one of the shadow creatures was gone. However, there was one more surprise.

Cat turned to talk to Veta and her eyes widened in amazement as Veta started to change in front of her. 'Your hair,' she said. 'Your eyes.'

Veta was no longer a grey, bedraggled creature. She was a girl just like Cat. And Zorb was an ordinary boy. It was the same everywhere they looked. The twilighters had returned to their original forms.

'You look just like us,' Tiger said.

'Yes,' Veta replied. 'Thanks to all of you. What can we do to repay you?'

'We came here for a reason,' Max said. 'A thought vial. Do you know of such a thing?'

'I think I might know what you seek,' Zorb said.

'Where is it?' Cat asked excitedly.

'Come with me,' Zorb told her. 'You'll see.'

They followed him across the hills. The sun was shining with an almost otherworldly clarity. Dormant trees and plants were beginning to awaken. Vast lakes shimmered in the sunlight.

'Our world is coming back to life,' Veta said. 'See how beautiful it is.'

'Yes,' Cat said, 'and not a patch of mist anywhere.'

Before long, they came to a huge, silver building.

'Is this it?' Max asked.

'This is where you will find the vial,' Zorb said. He led the way. 'This is our Hall of History. We are a nation of great stonemasons. We carve significant events in history into stone and create likenesses of all the most important people from our past.'

He showed them into a vast room.

'Wow, this place is awesome,' said Tiger, gazing at one of the carvings.

Zorb pointed to the stone face of a beautiful woman.

'Perlest,' said Ant.

'She visited us many, many years ago,' said Zorb. 'Look a little closer.'

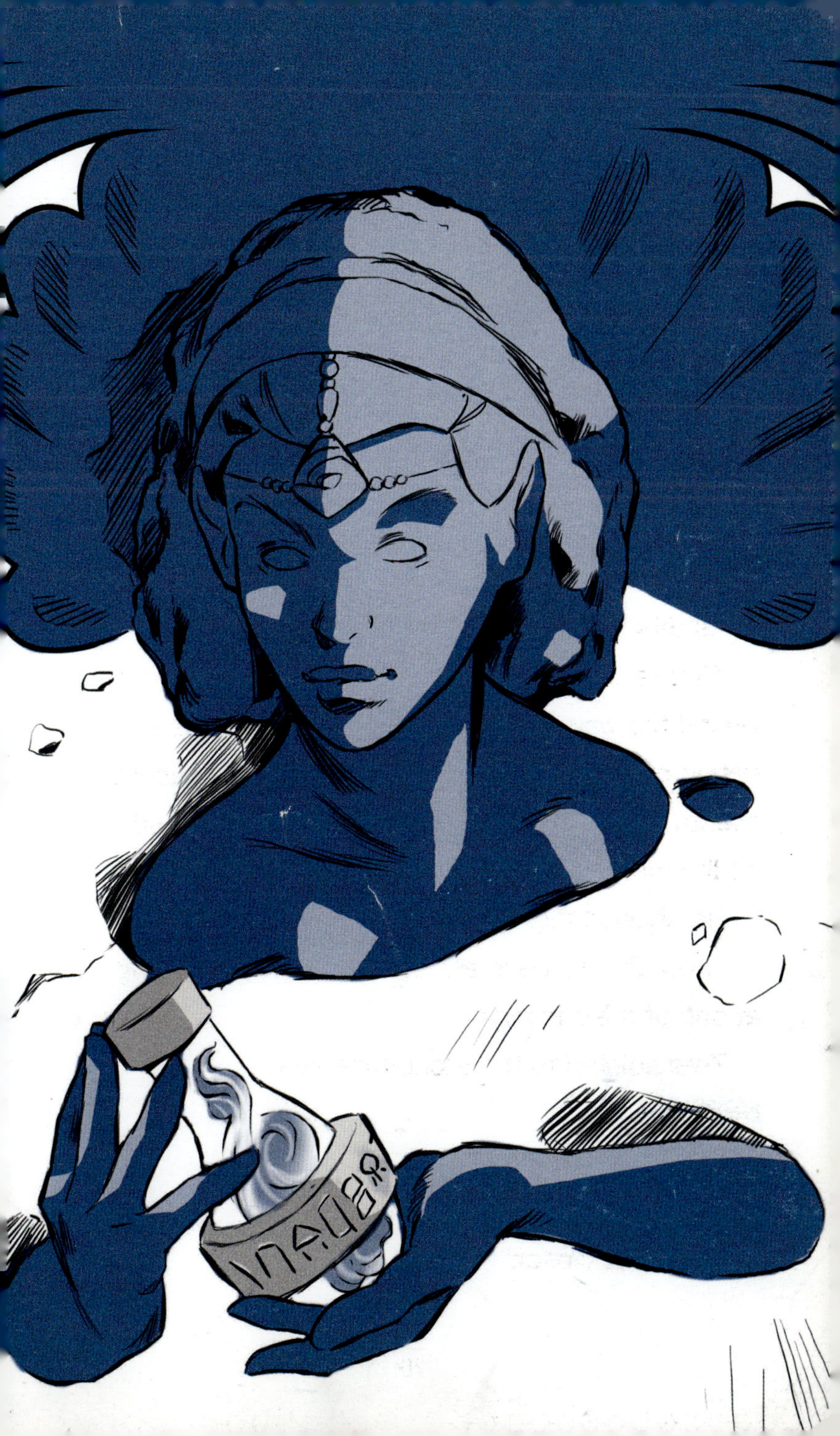

Max stepped forward. In the carving's hands was the vial they had been seeking. Max eased it out.

When he was done, the four friends started to turn the dials on their watches, ready to leave.

Zorb smiled. 'If you ever return, you will find four new carvings. We will make one of each of you to remember our victory.'

Max, Cat, Ant and Tiger waved as they prepared for their next rip-jump.

'To think', Veta said, 'we were once scared of our own shadows.'

'Not any more,' said Zorb with a smile.

NEXT ... Cries of the Parasings